Women of Asia

JOSEF BREITENBACH

Women of Asia

INTRODUCTION BY SPURGEON M. KEENY

THE JOHN DAY COMPANY New York

LIBRARY OF CONGRESS CATALOGUE CARD NUMBER: 68-8321

PHOTOGRAVURE ILLUSTRATIONS PRINTED BY D. H. GREAVES LTD, SCARBOROUGH, ENGLAND
TEXT PRINTED BY WILLIAM COLLINS SONS AND CO. LTD, COLLINS CLEAR-TYPE PRESS, LONDON AND GLASGOW
PRINTED IN GREAT BRITAIN

Introduction

Introduction

Josef Breitenbach became a person instead of a name to me when he dropped in to the U.N. to show me pictures he had taken in Korea. Some of these showed the work of the United Nations Children's Fund. Even I could see that they were the work of a real artist, and UNICEF made wide use of them. Since then Joe has visited Asia again and again in the employ of some great industry. In his busy life he has always found time to take pictures of women and children—and UNICEF is the richer for it.

Curiously enough, I never met Joe in Asia. When he was in Thailand or Japan I was in India or Afghanistan. But I came across his trail many times. Once, recently, it was in Bali, where a proud father showed me a picture of his little daughter in Balinese dancing costume Joe had taken. A week later a young Norwegian father who works for UNICEF brought out a whole album of wonderful shots by Joe of one of my favourite youngsters—tow-headed Tove. In my own office in Bangkok my young Chinese public information officer speaks with admiration approaching awe of what he learned from Joe about the art of taking pictures of plain people so that they come alive. You have seen plenty of pictures of Asian women. Probably they were the wives or daughters of Ambassadors or students coming to the West to attend universities. What you probably noticed was the splendour or the picturesqueness of the national costumes. If they were Indian women, your eye was probably caught by a caste mark or beauty spot on the forehead, the vermilion dye in the parting of the hair worn by a married woman, especially from Bengal, or (among the wealthier of South India) a diamond in the pierced nostril. Or, at the other end of the social scale, you may have seen pictures of some such oddity as the heavy ear-rings of the Dyaks of North Borneo, which stretch the lobes of the ears down to the shoulders.

Joe Breitenbach's pictures are of another kind. In this book you will see the ordinary Asian woman (sometimes a bit prettier than the average; for photographers are human). You will see her, not posed, but caught perhaps in a pause of her work. (She is nearly always working.) You will see her planting or harvesting rice or cooking or walking to market with her baby. You'll notice her costume of course, but most of all you'll notice her as a *person*.

Nevertheless, when Joe asked me to write something about the women of Asia 'to give a warm human background' to his pictures, I hesitated. I'm not a writer of the stature that Joe has as an artist. Also, I'm seldom in one place long enough to do anything but the things I have to do for UNICEF. On the other hand, I had wandered for eleven years in the countries where Joe had taken his pictures and I share his enthusiasm to make people in the West better acquainted with those of Asia, whom we have both come to admire and love. Hence the partnership.

7

Before we start to get acquainted with the average woman of Asia, we must understand clearly that in some ways she is sharply different from her sister in the West. First, she is not white nor does she care to be. A white person used to be semi-sacred in Asia; now he or she is just one more foreigner—richer perhaps and better educated than most Asian women, but often apparently unable to live away from a hotel or a house with electric lights, refrigerator, radio, and perhaps even air-conditioning. Secondly, the Asian woman is seldom a Christian. Usually she is Hindu, Muslim, or Buddhist or, among the 'tribes', the follower of a set of traditions and beliefs far older than those ancient religions. But in Asia one soon ceases to notice colour at all except for unusual variations. As for religion, we all live tolerantly together, respecting one another's taboos and cheerfully celebrating one another's holidays. (In Indonesia, the Muslims there observe not only Christmas but also Easter and Ascension Day, although Mohammed expressly taught his followers that Christ did not return from the dead. In short, one excuse for a holiday is as good as another.)

Clothing is as important to the Asian woman as to one of the West. In fact, it is one of the reasons why photographers are in paradise in Asia: there are no angles—only curves. The Indian sari, draped without a button, pin, or belt, comes nearest perfection in this respect. But the Chinese jacket and trousers, entirely different, have their own charm—and are more practical. The materials are silk for holidays if the wedding gifts ran to that; otherwise, and preferably of course for every day, cotton in every pattern and shade. Deep in the country one still sees cloth woven on hand looms in traditional patterns: but most people now wear cotton made in factories. Where Japan trades around the Indian Ocean even cotton often gives way to synthetics—for show but not for use.

Most women in Asia don't cover their heads except among the Muslims—and then not in Indonesia. In India, a corner of the sari used as a veil remains to remind us that the Hindu women too hid their faces, probably from the eyes of their Mogul conquerors. Also, one must not forget the hats worn in the fields from Taiwan to Burma. These are usually flat cones, perhaps a foot across, to keep off the sun—or even wider ones (up to two feet or more) to keep off the rain. I still remember the Vietnamese girls carrying bricks with their broad hats held on by chinstraps of wide blue ribbon. Recently, the road workers in Bali have blossomed out in shaped straw hats not unlike those worn by the Gibson girls in the U.S. at the turn of the century. Sometimes hats and veils are combined, as by the girls working among the sugar-cane in Taiwan. These are to prevent undue sunburn. (It seems that gentlemen there do prefer blondes—or an approximation thereof.)

Our woman of Asia of course likes jewellery too. There is far more variety than there is in even Western costume jewellery: but the fashions don't change every few years. Some of the styles are hundreds if not thousands of years old. The woman of India wears probably the most jewellery of anyone in Asia. Gold is of course preferred, but for the common woman it is largely out of reach except perhaps (among the Muslims) enough for a gold tooth. Silver is next, worn as necklaces, bracelets, and anklets. Silver money is not scorned; I've seen a sweeper bride in India with twenty-seven rupees twined in her hair. If silver is not to be had, brass will do. Nowadays the seller of plastic bracelets and anklets does a roaring business.

Farther east, the taste is for less but better jewellery. ('Roman' gold, 24 carat, is preferred.) In Bangkok little gold is worn except as chains. Our washerwoman, given the dollars to buy clothes for her new baby, brought the baby girl triumphantly the next day —naked as before but with a tiny gold bracelet around each wrist. A girl without a gold   8 chain is nothing in her circle. When she has saved a little money, she is off to the gold-smith's for her first thin, short chain. Later it grows longer and has a pendant. As soon as she can afford it, she trades the chain for a thicker one, losing about ten per cent of the value, but rising more than that in the eyes of her jealous friends, who appraise the new chain by weight as they hold it in their palms.

Lipstick, in Asia, is for city girls—but the city need not be large. In fact, wherever movies are shown one is likely to see a few girls with lips redder than God made them. Burmese girls seem particularly prone to depart from the ancient ways. Many are just youngsters having their fling but, as the movie circle widens (with its fifteen minutes of advertising between shows) more and more girls wonder whether they couldn't scrape together the few *kyats* or *baht* to buy one of those tempting sticks of colour. Of course, a bit of colouring from the juice of certain flowers has been common for centuries, especially in China. This was applied not only to the lips but to the fingernails. Rouge too has been used—often under the eyes rather than on the cheeks.

Few Asian women outside towns smoke. (I was much surprised recently in Bali to be asked for a cigarette by a girl of sixteen working on the road.) But, in tobacco-growing countries, such as Burma, when a woman takes to smoking, she does so with a vengeance. She smokes, not a cigarette, but a green cheroot thicker than the thickest cigar and from eight inches to a foot long. (I'm a smoker myself but I shudder when, at dawn before breakfast, I see an innocent-looking girl puffing contentedly on one of those green horrors.) Sometimes, in the old-fashioned family circle, a jumbo cheroot up to two feet long is suspended by a string in the middle of the group, so that everybody can take a puff in turn.

More frequently, women chew betel nut, which makes their saliva red and their teeth black. But this custom seems to be slowly dying and with it the dentist's trade of fitting black false teeth to match the real ones. In Taiwan women (and men) have a passion for chewing salted black watermelon seeds. In shelling the thin and slippery seed, the Taiwanese show a delicate skill that squirrels might envy.

With notable exceptions, such as the Chinese 'sworn spinsters', girls look forward to marriage as the great event in their lives. Parents too give the matter months and years of thought: for in many countries the girl must bring a dowry. If a father has half a dozen daughters, the cost of marrying them all off will hang over his head like the spectre of the mortgage on the farm in an old-fashioned American melodrama.

Marriages used to be arranged by the parents of the couple, with no foolishness about romantic love. They still are in many if not most cases. Among the Chinese, the 'go-between' has always played her role—for a commission on the dowry. One of her important jobs was to see to it that the bride and groom sat down on the marriage bed at the same instant to assure that neither would dominate the other.

But the days are nearly gone when the girl never saw her future husband until the marriage ceremony. Nowadays she usually manages to have a good look at him and to learn quite a bit about him. If she doesn't like what she sees or hears, she is quite capable of saying that he is not for her. Sometimes she wins.

The marriage and following feast are on a staggering scale. Relatives and friends come and camp for anything up to a week. The bill is usually paid by the groom's father, who may go into debt for years to put on a good show. Papa must also pay, at least in India, for a number of saris specified in the marriage agreement.

The marriage ceremony itself varies greatly, depending on whether the couple are Hindu, Muslim, or Buddhist. Whatever they are, there will be plenty of flowers, usually 9 worn around the neck as garlands. In Thailand the ceremony is a thing of lovely simplicity. After the couple have taken their vows, they are tied together with a string symbolizing the bonds that now hold them. Then they kneel before a little table with their hands outstretched over silver basins. The wedding guests file past and pour lustral water on the hands in blessing of the new union.

The bride has two problems of adjustment; to live with her husband—and with his mother. In many countries, especially China, the latter is the bigger problem. Timidly the bride will show what she knows about cooking, keeping the house tidy inside and out, and managing money. I know of one Indian girl who became the apple of her mother-in-law's eye because she was especially skilful in drawing the designs with which every Indian house is decorated on the feast of *Holi*. If the bride is wise, she will ask her mother-in-law for advice. In any case she will get it. If she listens carefully, she will pick up valuable tips on the likes and dislikes of her husband and how to get around him. If things go well, the two women will form a silent partnership to manage all the men of the house.

The blessing of the new home in Thailand is also a time for special ceremony. (When this is to be is of course decided by the astrologer, who fixes not only the day but the hour and minute.) Then the priests come in their saffron robes, and there is another party, with food and drink for all. The main purpose of the ceremony is to protect the house and the people in it from harm. This the priests do by stretching a string around the compound, putting three white dots to form a triangle above each doorway, and saying the magic words that will keep the evil spirits from passing into the house.

The house in the rural areas is a much simpler building than in the West. In most places in Asia the problem is heat, not cold, and the builder thinks first of ventilation. In Thailand, in the country, the house is a sketchy affair with a bamboo frame, woven palm leaves as siding, and thatch for a roof. In the river valleys at least it will be raised on stilts up to ten or more feet high to be safe when the floods come and also to catch the breeze. In other countries where bamboo is not to be had, the building material may be burnt brick if there is money enough; otherwise (and usually) it is made of sun-dried brick or simply packed earth with a coating of lime to keep the earth from washing away in the first rain. There are seldom glass windows, and all too seldom enough of any kind: windows are where thieves come in. The family, often underfed, also consider intense cold what you and I would call a pleasant breeze. (This lack of ventilation is one reason for so much TB.)

The house is often tiny, but it is seldom crowded. When everybody sits, eats, and sleeps on the floor not much furniture is needed. A few cooking pots, a few mats for bedding, a few clothes, and a shrine make up the lot—not more than the family can carry if they move.

Every household must have water—and few villages have it piped in. The exceptions are where there is plenty of bamboo, which by local ingenuity can be made into quite acceptable pipes. It usually comes from the village well. In India there used to be two: one for the upper classes and one for the outcasts who were called by Gandhi *harijans*, meaning 'the children of God'. Now most villages are learning that it is better to have one good well than two bad ones. In many places there is not even one well for the whole village, but the water comes from irrigation ditches or from a pond where the rain-water collects—and in which the buffaloes wallow too. If the wife boils the water, everything is all right; if she doesn't (because she doesn't know about germs), she will help spread water-borne diseases, which cause perhaps half the deaths, especially of children, in Asia.

One of the woman's main jobs in life is to carry water—at least until her children get big enough to do so. She is at it from dawn to dark. What she doesn't have to use at 10 once she pours into a big earthen jar standing somewhere in the shade, called Shanghai jars in China, Java jars in Indonesia, and klong jars in Thailand. If she could get piped water into the house, her work would be cut by at least a quarter.

Cooking too takes a lot of time. The Asian housewife doesn't snap on a switch and set the dial for temperature and time. She doesn't even cook in the house except sometimes when it is raining heavily. Then she fills the house and her eyes with smoke because the windows are few and you need a hole in the roof for smoke to come out: unfortunately rain also comes in. In fine weather she cooks outdoors over a little fire of charcoal if there is wood in the neighbourhood. If she knows her business and has something to cook with, she can turn out a meal that will not only satisfy hungry workers from the rice field but will rival the sad stuff from most restaurants. In India, where there is usually no charcoal, she uses dried cow-dung, a reserve supply of which is always drying on the side walls of the house or garden wall, skilfully smacked against the wall in handy-sized pancakes.

Every family knows that it must have water, but by no means every family feels in need of a privy. They do as their ancestors have always done—go to the fields. Every morning and evening in India you will see a little knot of women modestly setting out along the well-marked path to the fields carrying their brass jugs of water instead of toilet paper. Health educators tell them all this is very bad, but the habits of a lifetime are hard to break. One reason is that 'going to the fields' is not only necessary but, next to the bathing hour, it is the social event of the day. It gives a woman a chance to get away from her children and her chores and have a lively gossip with her cronies. A more practical point: in most of India privies may be cleaned only by a special class of persons, who may not be available even if they can be afforded. As a result, it is extraordinarily difficult to get latrines built for every house in the village. In one 'demonstration area' outside Calcutta a concentrated effort has been going on for twenty-five years, but three-quarters of the people still go to the fields.

Our average woman keeps her family on earnings of not much more than one U.S. dollar a week per person for everything. Many people say lightly, 'Oh, but things are much cheaper in the East.' As a matter of fact, the main food, rice, does not cost much less than it does in the West. The result is that at least three-quarters of what the family earns goes into food. As we have seen, heating the house costs nothing, which is just as well. Rent too is a small item in the village because nearly every family has its own hut. Something must be spent on clothing, but I know a fairly typical family in Indonesia that spends an average of one U.S. dollar a year per person for this item.

If the family owns a bit of land, it will get along unless the crop fails. If that happens, the family goes into debt. All too often the interest rate is ruinous—from 50 to 100 per cent a year. Unless the debt can be paid off in a few months, the family may be enslaved for life.

If the family has no land, it can't borrow money from strangers at any rate, for it can offer no security. Then the thin gold chains are sold, and after that the family must go hungry until another job is found, in merciless competition. The only other solution is help from relatives, which is usually given if possible; for family ties are stronger in Asia than in the West.

In fact, how the Asian woman manages her budget remains something of a mystery to me. I tried once in East Pakistan to work out the budget of a family of five that I picked at random. I failed and decided to try with a second family. That one turned out to have nine persons. But the fact that the income is tiny doesn't keep the family from having plenty of children. The average woman of thirty will have three or more living and   11 probably one or two dead—usually of malaria or some intestinal disease. Now that malaria is being cleared out of Asia there will be more babies than ever.

The Asian mother can't pack off her children to day nurseries and kindergartens: she has them with her always. Joe Breitenbach's pictures show how she carries them for the first year or so. The methods are two: one, used by the Japanese and Chinese, in which the baby fits into a big pocket on the mother's back in cold weather and is neatly strapped on in warm weather by a cloth which is tied at the bottom around the mother's waist and at the top around her shoulders or across her chest. The other system used is to carry the child on the mother's hip. Seldom in Asia do you see a child carried in the mother's arms. Those arms have other things to do: usually one of them is busy balancing two or even three jars of water on her head.

The difficult period is when the child is crawling or just learning to walk. The busy mother can't keep an eye on him all the time so that she often fastens a small bell on him, which announces when he is in motion and where.

The Asian mother is unusually fond of her children. If the family has enough to eat, life flows smoothly, especially in Buddhist countries. Parents are gentle, and one hears very few small fry yelling because of bad temper. If the parents die, or a poor family has too many children, the extras often go to live with cousins or aunts by informal adoption. In some countries, such as Thailand, when a girl has a baby before marriage, the parents may raise a row with the girl, but neither they, nor the neighbours, nor the law take it out on the innocent baby. In effect, there are no illegitimate children in Thailand.

Most of Asia lives primarily on rice. This is grown wherever there is enough water. Elsewhere, especially to the north, the rice gives way to wheat. There are also other grains such as millet and barley, and, in a relatively few places, maize. Too few beans and peas are grown, and far too few vegetables, so that the family is usually short of vitamins and protein. Great parts of Asia, especially in India and Indonesia, are the most poorly nourished in the world, for their food is not only less in quantity, it is lower in quality than in the West.

In the average Asian home life revolves around the rice crop. Planting seedlings one by one is largely woman's work—one of the most tiring forms of stoop-labour in the world. She does it uncomplainingly, in water half-way up to her knees, and frequently with her baby on her back. Otherwise, the child is parked in a dry spot in the shade next to the flooded rice field.

The harvest of the rice crop is a time of joy if the crop has been good. The rice is harvested plant by plant, bound into little sheaves, and often carried home on the head of the reaper. Then it is stripped from the stalk and, later, hulled. This is done in Indonesia by pounding the rice in a log hollowed out for the purpose. This is usually a job for one strong woman, but sometimes for company's sake two work together. They pound out the rice to intricate tunes: one can hear the sound of their beating from half a mile away.

These habits are gradually changing with the coming of small rice mills with petrol-driven motors. The result is a polished rice, which looks lovely but which has lost most of its vitamins. But the people *will* eat white rice: it's the fashion. In Malaysia it has been found that nutrition improves and the dreaded disease of beri-beri disappears when the rubber harvest is bad: if people are poorer and can't afford white rice, they eat cheaper unpolished rice instead—and are the healthier for it.

A woman's life is thus made up of an unending round of cooking, carrying water, and looking after the children and the domestic animals. Of course, as soon as the children grow to be five or six they pitch in and help. One of the everyday sights of Asia is that of 12 a very small boy or girl perched on a huge water buffalo headed for the nearest pond. There the animal will sink down contentedly into the water until only the nostrils and horns stick out, along with enough of the back to keep the child's seat dry. If the animal sinks a little too low it is all part of the game.

The mother doesn't have much time for sewing—and not much need for it. In the tropics, boys run naked until they are five or six. The girls are more modest and wear a cloth around the middle from the age of three or four. Even the adults have few garments that require sewing. The women's garments in India, for example, often require no sewing at all. There are no socks to mend because none are worn. In many places, however, elaborate knitting and embroidery is done. Sometimes this is traditional, but often it has been introduced by missionaries, to help the family earn a little more cash. Some of the embroidery, especially from China, is extraordinarily fine, and is the joy of tourists.

No sketch of an Asian household is complete without a mention of its pets. I should place first the water buffalo except that that ungainly animal is more a member of the family than a pet. Every country child, boy or girl, looks forward to the day when he or she can take the family buffalo out for a graze and a wallow.

Next come dogs, whose ancestry usually won't bear examination. By day they play with the children; by night they bark challenges to neighbour dogs or howl at the moon just as they do in the West. They have every reason to be mournful: scraps are not plentiful in a poor family, and the dogs must find their food where they can. Among the worst-looking ones in Asia are those in Buddhist countries, where, for religious reasons, the owners won't destroy the dogs they don't want but also too often don't feed them.

Cats seem to me less plentiful than on American farms, but no country is without them. In Thailand the favourite is not the Siamese with the scrannel voice so prized in the upper levels of Western society, but the bigger one from up-country in Korat.

As for the rest, the range is enormous—from mongoose to talking birds. In our house in Bangkok, in addition to dogs and cats, we have pigeons, a duck, and a gibbon—known to the servants as 'the thief' because of her skill in stealing anything eatable. She has recently adopted two half-grown kittens, which she picks up by the neck with either hand or foot. Then she takes one for a wild run over the rooftops while the other patiently waits its turn.

Most Asian women love flowers and grow them if they can. Except in Japan, flowers are little used for house decoration, but are picked in great quantities to make the garlands that are used to welcome guests and for all kinds of festivities.

The Asian woman and her husband are the soul of hospitality. No matter how poor the village one visits, there will always be at least whatever fruit is in season and a coconut with the end chopped off to provide a sweet drink. If they have advance notice, they will turn out an astonishing assortment of sweets, usually very sticky and beloved of flies. (It had been hoped that the widespread use of D.D.T. would kill all the flies in Asia. Flies, however, are hardier than mosquitoes. After three years they positively thrive on D.D.T.) But these little things don't interfere with hospitality. If there is a bit of mosquito net around, it is thrown over the sweet. If there is not, a palm leaf keeps the flies on the move.

Several times a year in every country the whole routine of life is broken while everybody takes time out for special holidays. In the Muslim countries, prominent is the end of the month-long fast, *Ramadan*. Among the Hindus the high-jinks take place at *Diwali*, the Festival of Lights, and *Holi*. In preparation for the Festival of Lights there is a tremendous cleaning up, washing of all the walls of the house, and drawing with crayon elaborate designs at each threshold. The reason for all this tidiness is that the goddess of the   13 household, Lakshmi, the goddess of good luck, will not enter a house that is dirty. *Holi* is a much more rowdy holiday, when the younger people throw red powder on one another and on passing strangers as well. In Burma (and in parts of Thailand, Cambodia, and Vietnam) there is the Water Festival, when they devote five days to pouring pails of water on one another when they are least expecting it. During these periods it is useless to expect any work from anybody. The best thing to do is to close the office or the shop and go and throw water also.

The Asian woman likes to sing if she has a good voice—and sometimes even if she hasn't. For many women, singing makes up in part for the reading that they don't do. Here tradition plays a large role: one may hear the ancient hymns of the Vedas or songs to the gods on appropriate holidays. Or the song may celebrate the glories of some hero of the *Ramayana* or any one of a hundred folk epics. Or it may be one in praise of love or beauty or a simple lullaby.

Sometimes the songs are not so old as the hearers may think. I recall hearing a bride singing in India. When I asked the Indian nurses with me what the words were, I was told that they didn't understand themselves: they were probably thousands of years old in a dialect that only the sweepers understood. Then one of the younger nurses spoke up timidly; 'I understand it. She is singing in Gujerati.'

'What is she saying?'

'O young man with the bright eyes on the motor-bike, don't ride so fast. If you go slower, you may see the light in my eyes—and want to stop.'

Some places, such as Bengal, are especially rich in songs and have their favourite song-writers, such as Tagore, who wrote in this century, but who is already part of Bengal's life. In the more 'advanced' countries, such as India and Japan, movie hits sweep the country just as they do in the West. Sometimes the influence comes from overseas. When I asked a bright young miss who had been singing Burmese songs to me who her favourite singer was, she replied: 'Elvis Presley.'

The Asian woman has more than her share of superstitions. Her belief in astrology would not even be counted a superstition in most Asian countries, where even many of the educated look on it as a science. Palmistry has a lower place, but is very popular. As for the thousand and one other beliefs, they used to be looked on by foreigners with dislike—possibly because they were different from Western superstitions, which are still plentiful. Nowadays, there is a tendency to encourage traditional beliefs that make for better health and to ignore all the rest that don't do actual harm. If a Balinese mother wants to draw a cross on the top of her baby's head, let her do so if the paint doesn't harm the baby's skin. If a Pakistani birth attendant wants to open all the doors in the house in order that the baby may come out more easily, why not? But if the old wives of Burma tell a preg-nant woman that she must starve herself in order that the baby may not be too large, then it is time to teach the woman better, lest she become anaemic and the baby's life be endangered. Also, if a birth attendant in the Philippines wants to use one of the father's dirty shirts to press against the newly cut umbilical cord, action is necessary—or lockjaw may be the result of an attempt to assure that the father will love the baby.

The Asian mother knows all too well what it means to have sickness in the family. In the past her loved ones would almost certainly have the chills and fevers of malaria and, from time to time, would also be swept by smallpox and perhaps cholera. One in five babies still dies before reaching one year, and the whole period up to five is one of peril. If they survive the first five years, they usually live to normal old age. But, except in Japan, life expectancy on the average in Asia is still only little more than half that in the West. 14

When sickness comes, the mother usually cannot reach or pay for a doctor and must rely on the local herbalist, who sometimes helps but usually doesn't. Nature itself must cure the patient if there is to be a cure. This situation, however, is slowly changing. With the assistance of the World Health Organization and UNICEF, 20,000 health centres (mostly for mothers and children) have been established in Asia, and the number is rising by 2,000 a year. These look after the urgent health needs of some 75 million people. But that is only one-tenth of the total—not counting China. What Asia needs, as much as anything else, is more trained doctors, nurses, and midwives who are willing to work in the villages.

The birth of a baby in Asia is not a crisis: it is taken as a matter of course. A trained midwife in the Philippines told me of her first call to attend an Igorot woman in the mountains of Luzon. When she arrived at the house the door was locked and no one answered. She peeked through a hole in the matting wall and saw the woman squatted over a pile of fresh wood ashes. Soon the baby popped out and fell into the ashes. Then the mother cheerfully called out: 'Come in!'

'Why didn't you let me help before?'

'I didn't need any help. But I thought it would be nice to have you cut and tie the cord. I wanted a midwife to do this; I hear it's the fashion now.'

Four out of five babies in Asia are born with only the help of the village traditional birth attendant or of another member of the family. These women usually have plenty of experience, some of which they'd like to forget. With UNICEF aid, some 50,000 of them have received elementary instruction on cleanliness and on the need to call for help in complicated deliveries. This network still reaches only ten per cent of the women but it is rapidly widening. The average woman's chances for a safe delivery are getting better every year.

Death comes all too often to the Asian household. If it is that of a child, it is taken with something of the fatalism that was common in Western life a century ago: one had to expect to lose two or three out of a half dozen or more. But behind that impassive front is the same mother love in Asia as elsewhere. At a clinic in Java I happened to overhear a mother's plea: 'Please, doctor, save this one for me. All the rest have died of fever (malaria), and now this one is hot too.'

Everyone who has spent even a few months in Asia has passed the pathetic little processions on foot behind four men carrying a coffin or perhaps a covered figure on a couple of boards. They were on the way to the cemetery or to the place of cremation. In India the body is burnt, preferably on the bank of a holy river, and the ashes sprinkled on the water. In Java the graves are covered with roofs several feet off the ground, like tiny houses. The Chinese burn paper models or pictures of all the things the spirit will need in the next world: food, furniture, money—and, in these modern days—an automobile. Those who saw the film, *The World of Suzie Wong*, will remember that the dead child carried with him to the spirit world even a letter of recommendation.

A widow usually has a hard time in Asia. If her husband dies after the children are mostly grown up, she will usually be looked after: one of the reasons for wanting many sons is to guard against just such a calamity. But, if the children are small, she and they will probably become absorbed in the 'extended family' of her parents. If her relations with her mother-in-law have been good, she may still do all right; otherwise, she is likely to become the household drudge.

If she tries to make her own way, she may succeed if the family owns a bit of land. If not, she has to compete with men at common labour, where she will be paid about a 15 fourth less than a man even though she is often a better worker. If she has had a bit of education, she can probably get work as a teacher or a nurse, for which the demand is greater than the supply.

As badly off as the women of Asia are, they are catching glimpses of a better way of life, and are determined to have some of it for their children. The washerwoman at our house is illiterate but she has learned far more English while she has worked for us than I have learned Thai. In our family pidgin she puts the case thus: 'I no go school. My papa, mamma, very poor. I wash clothes till I die. But my little girl go school. Want work office, write letters.'

This is what the professors call 'the revolution in expectations'. How is it coming about?

The main reason for the change is very simple: most of the countries of Asia have won their independence in the last fifteen years. What impressed many observers most was that daily life in many countries became even more difficult than before. What got less notice were the new constitutions, many patterned closely on that of the United States, most of which at a stroke gave equal rights to women. In India, where the woman had always 'belonged' to someone—her father until marriage, then her husband, and possibly her son in her old age—the change is tremendous. She is learning that she is a *person*, with her own rights. To make these brave new phrases real will of course take many years, but the pattern is laid down. Step by step girls will go to school in the same percentage as boys. Women will gradually get the same rights as men in marriage, in property holding, in voting. Even now millions of women are casting their ballots who can't read but who recognize their parties by the pictures on the paper.

With the new governments came a new crop of politicians who promised (as politicians often do) more than they could deliver. But the very fact that they promised them, in thousands of speeches, has helped to build up the expectations.

One of the promises was more schools, and this promise is generally being kept as fast as new schools can be built and teachers trained. The schools of Indonesia are working two and even three shifts. The teachers in training are three times what they were ten years ago. In India, compulsory primary education is fast coming into force. Among India's more than 500 million people, thirteen boys out of forty of school age go to school but only five out of forty girls. In the next five years, however, the number of girls entering school will be 8.5 million as compared with 6 million boys.

Along with the schools are coming the health services, with their public health nurses and, especially, the midwives. These workers really touch the village and are being enthusiastically received. The children of our average woman are being protected from smallpox, cholera, tuberculosis, and several other communicable diseases. Malaria is going with all the fever, wretchedness, and death it brought—and yaws, with its dreadful sores, is almost a thing of the past. Everybody in the village wants an injection now. Better health will bring savings with which to pay for the children's school books.

Another influence on our average woman, even though she be from the country, is the cinema, which is now reaching even quite small towns and, open-air style, even the larger villages. Here she sees life in other lands, usually glorified and often otherwise distorted, but always with people wearing good clothes and surrounded by gadgets that she soon comes to recognize—and want.

Nor must we forget the radio, which one can hear just as plainly as others even if one has never learned to read. True, the village household seldom has a radio, but one of the first purchases the tiniest shopkeeper makes is a small but loud one. The Chinese, 16 especially, seem never happier than when a whole streetful of radios are on full blast, preferably on different stations. In Afghanistan, too, I was astonished on a recent visit to find a transistor radio in almost every village headman's house I visited. As the radio comes in, the story-teller, popular throughout the ages, goes out.

Included too must be commercial advertisements, with pictures, so that even the illiterate may dream of owning the tempting things that are offered. Our average woman is beginning to dream that she too may one day be wearing a lovely dress and shiny shoes, with a wrist-watch.

Let's look ahead twenty-five years. By then our average woman will have yielded the stage to her daughter, now six. How will the daughter be different from her mother?

She will still be poor, and will probably not have much more money for groceries than her mother had. But she will make better use of that money, for she will know much more about the variety of foods the family should eat and will be growing some of the protective foods in her own garden. She will perhaps have learned about foods in such a project as UNICEF and UNESCO are sponsoring in Thailand to include more nutrition and health in the curriculum of primary teachers and to get the teachers working with the villages to improve them. The results will be seen in house gardens, in improved wells, in privies, and in better housekeeping in the whole village. The daughter's children will have much better health than those of today.

All of the other influences I've mentioned will have been at work too. The daughter will probably learn to read, and will absorb the new influence all the faster, especially when she gets electric light in her house, as she probably will.

But over this cheerful scene hangs one dark cloud: the rapid increase of population resulting from better health services. At the present rate, the population of Asia will double within thirty-five years. Food production may keep pace for that time, but what about the thirty-five years after that?

Here are two great forces in conflict; the pressure of population growth and the desire for a better life. It took England 130 years to stabilize its population. On the other hand, by drastic measures, Japan did it in ten. How to do it must be decided by each country for itself. India's campaign is under way, as is Pakistan's. If these and other overcrowded countries succeed in holding their populations at a point where they can feed them and give them a little margin for saving, our average woman's future—and her daughter's—is bright.

SPURGEON M. KEENY
Director for Asia 1950-63, UNICEF

The Map

The Captions

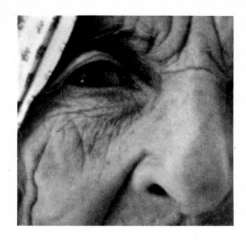

1 Persian grandmother. Teheran, Iran, 1962.

2 On the way to Teheran, 1964. Woman in her black chador on donkey, followed by her young son.

3 Windy day. Isfahan, Iran, 1962. Mother in black and daughter in white chador in the former Persian capital. In Teheran western dress is mostly worn; in other cities and in the villages, women—even young ones—still wear the old attire.

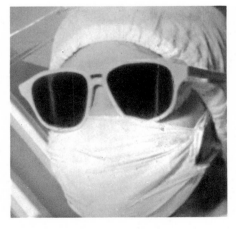

4 Penicillin comes to Persia. Teheran, Iran, 1960. Modern pharmaceutical plant: Persian girls filling penicillin bottles under aseptic conditions.

5 Waiting for her turn at the well. On the Outskirts of Delhi, India, 1957.

6 Beauty at work. Bombay, India, 1960. Most of the heavy work is done by women. Yet they still have the grace of a dancer in body and movement and in the exquisite colour combinations of their saris.

7 A little at a time and all together. Bombay, India, 1960. Gangs of women transport excavated earth as it might have been done two thousand years ago. They fill the basket, walk a hundred yards or so, throw the earth into a heap, walk back and repeat the chore hundreds of times. This earns them twenty cents a day. There is violent opposition to the introduction of bulldozers, which could multiply efficiency more than a thousand times.

8 Baby gets his bath. Borsul, Bengal, 1957. After the saris are washed baby enjoys his daily bath. At this season 'cold' water has the temperature of a hot bath.

9 A doctor in the village. Nasrapur, India, 1957. In this village near Poona the government-appointed doctor often treats as many as a hundred patients a day from all the surrounding countryside. Here a shepherd's family (shepherds wear red turbans) worry about their sick baby.

10 Indian village near Puri, in Orissa, 1957. Each family lives in a straw-thatched mud hut with walls nearly three feet thick: it is cool inside. The outer and inner walls are ornamented by frescoes executed in mineral colours by the women of the household. About every three months they scratch everything off for the holidays and renew it entirely.

11 Pattern of life. Inside the same house. Geometric forms are interwoven with realistic ones in the old tradition to create the great tale of life.

12 Housewife outside Calcutta chopping wood for the kitchen stove. Bengal, India, 1960.

27

13 On a road in Orissa. India, 1957. One of the few modern roads in India, near Bhubaneswar, lined with shadow-giving bodhi trees.

14 She sells everything the village needs. Indian general store at Nasrapur, a traditional village of several hundred inhabitants near Poona, some eighty miles south-east of Bombay, 1957.

15 Young girl at the market. Karachi, Pakistan, 1957.

16 Kathmandu, Nepal, 1964. Young Nepalese woman sitting outside a temple on the city market.

17 Nepalese home, 1964. A public health nurse of Indian origin and dress helps the mother with advice on hygiene and assistance in nutrition and cooking problems. Infant mortality in Nepal is largely caused by wrong feeding.

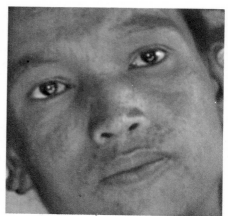

18 'Can you help my child?' Nepal, 1964. Mother with vitamin-deficient child at the health centre in Patan, which was installed in 1964 by the Nepalese Government in co-operation with UNICEF.

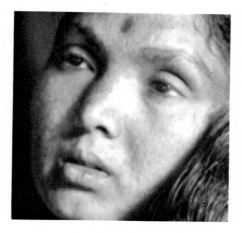

19 Patan, Nepal, 1964. Mother with two sickly children visiting the newly installed health centre.

20 A little shop in Kathmandu, Nepal, 1964. The woman owner of a small rice and grocery store. The mountain country between India and Tibet was practically inaccessible to Westerners until aeroplane connection was established a few years ago. Life in cities and in villages is still very much as it might have been three hundred years ago.

21 Woman harnessing a horse. Rangoon, Burma, 1958. Outside the Shwedagon pagoda.

22 Begging woman and child outside the main post office. Colombo, Ceylon, 1960.

23 Panning for tin. Kuala Lumpur, Malaysia, 1957. Malaysia is the greatest tin producer in the world. Tin is mined three different ways: with big dredges, with powerful jets of water, and as here (the old way), with wooden bowls, panned very much as gold was in the early days. The sand is washed away and the heavy metal remaining in the bowl is emptied into buckets, which gradually fill up.

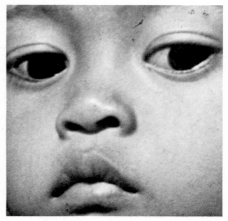

24 Mother and child. Near Jakarta, Java, 1960.

25 Telling a story of long ago. Bali, 1960. Different kinds of dances are performed in the villages of this small island, often all day long or through the night until dawn. The great gamlang orchestra furnishes the music for this pantomimic saga of the Ramayana. Beautiful gold-painted dresses and jewellery shining in the sun lend themselves to the sinuous movements of the body; the dancer's hands flutter like butterflies or leaves in the wind.

26 Start at sunrise. Bali, 1960. Mother and daughter going to the market at six o'clock in the morning. They carry on their heads ceramic cooking-pots to be sold; these are artfully bound together.

27 Dancer famous at twelve, performing the classical Kebyar. Klungkung, Bali, 1960. Bali is one small island of the three thousand which make up Indonesia. It is Hindu while the others are Moslem, and its culture is distinctly different. Music and dance are alive in every village and of an infinite variety. In all classical dances only young girls perform; they stop as soon as puberty is reached.

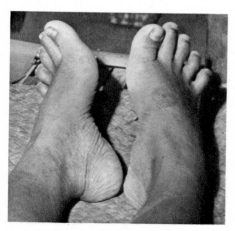

28 Baby's first bath. Bali, 1960. A visiting nurse service has been organized by the Indonesian Government to reduce infant mortality. The stone house built around a bamboo pole has an elevated sleeping area with a big mat made from palm leaves. Old, clean cotton clothes are used as diapers.

29 Bali mother wearing the traditional batik sarong, 1960. In spite of government prohibition women show their breasts as their mothers did: they would not show their ankles, however. Mothers think the baby needs a cap even in the hottest weather.

30 Thai silk in the making. Upper Thailand, near Korat, 1957. Nearly all women in the villages weave silk from thread to the final cloth. Sitting on the elevated dais and the straw mat which is the sleeping-place, this woman is winding the silk thread.

31 Home on the river. Bangkok, Thailand, 1965. On the Chao Phya river, which runs through Bangkok, barges and boats of all descriptions are the permanent abode and livelihood of families.

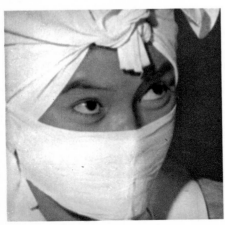

32 Keeping the germs away from baby. Bangkok, Thailand, 1963. Sathorn Hospital has a service which provides home visiting nurses for the first week or two after a baby is born.

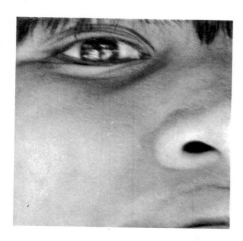

33 Cambodia, 1962. Near Siem Réap outside Angkorvat. Cambodians have a light brown skin, different from other Asians. The hand-woven toga-like cotton dress leaves the shoulders free and goes down to the ankles. It is supplemented by a shawl over one shoulder.

34 They wash their clothes and gossip. Village women doing the laundry and bathing in a pond outside the village. Laguna Province, Luzon, Philippines, 1958.

35 Philippine girl of about fourteen, ready to cut sugarcane. Bulacaan Province, Luzon, 1966. At harvesttime groups of six to ten women of all ages between thirteen and sixty travel as teams along the road to look for temporary work in sugar plantations. This girl is wearing the long red gloves to protect herself against the cutting edges of the sugar-cane leaves.

36 Evening cigar with grandson. In a small village of the Bontoc tribe in the Mountain Province, Northern Philippines, 1958. The houses are made of woven palm leaves and wood, thatched with straw.

33

37 Tattoo Blouse.   Mountain Province, Northern Philippines, 1958. Blue tattoo on the gold-brown skin replaces the blouse; the whole dress consists of a white and red handwoven square of cotton draped as a skirt, and a necklace of beads.

38 Her grandfather was a head-hunter.   Philippines, 1958. Igorot mother in the mountainous country of North Luzon, near Banaue.

39 Harvest time in the Rice Terrace Country, Philippines, 1958.   This girl from the Ifugao tribe is not wearing a wig but twenty pounds of rice which she is bringing uphill: the hands carry buckets and tools. The blouse is a concession to missionary influence.

40 They like their teacher. Boys' class in a city school. Saigon, Vietnam, 1962. Wherever I went in Vietnam the school teachers seemed to me wonderfully kind and sensitive women, achieving a very warm and understanding relationship with their pupils.

34

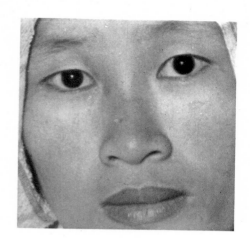

41 Vietnamese mother. Saigon, 1962.

42 Mother of five learns to shoot. Vietnam, 1962. Army Training Centre, Binh tu Dong, outside Saigon. Para-military cadres for women were organized in 1958 by Madame Ngo Dinh Nhu, sister-in-law of the then Vietnam President Diem, as 'National Women's Solidarity Movement'. The youthful marksman in front is the thirty-year-old wife of a city official.

43 Young Vietnamese secretary at the Government Office of Taxes and Revenues in Saigon operates a computer. 1962. The outer slit skirt contrasts in colour with the silk trousers.

44 Modern Vietnamese family. Outside Saigon, 1962.

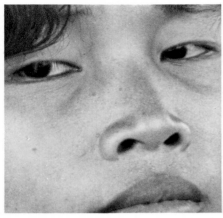

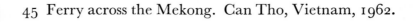
45 Ferry across the Mekong. Can Tho, Vietnam, 1962.

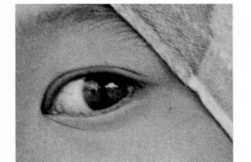

46 Young Vietnamese girl, Saigon, 1962. The becoming wide hats are worn mainly to preserve the light complexion.

47 Elder sister taking little brother for a ride, Hongkong, 1965. Lascar Row, business street in the old Chinese district.

48 Hongkong, 1966. In Aberdeen on the south coast of the island behind Mount Victoria lives an entirely Chinese population on twenty thousand junks and sampans. They are mainly fishermen with their families. Coming ashore, they wear the traditional satin suits. The big tubs may contain salted fish or sea-food and are marked with the name of the owner.

49 Chinese rice fields, 1961, in the 'New Territories', the British-administered coastal strip between Kowloon and the Chinese People's Republic. Two women rest on the way to market: their wide hats consist of the brim only with a curtain-like black fringe, a distinctive feature of the regional dress.

50 Shatin, 1963. In the 'New Territories', leased in 1898 by the British Government, life goes on pretty much as in old China. This is a country fair with festivities and sacrifices to the ancestors. The writing on the banner gives the name of the sponsoring organization: Teh Shan Shou Chin—something like Virtue and Kindness Club.

51 Ready for work or play. Taiwan, 1963. Farm woman working in the rice fields near Pingtung. In spite of the great heat, or perhaps as a protection against it, she is all wrapped up in a padded coat, as in severe winter.

52 In the rain waiting for a bus. Taipei, Taiwan, 1966.

53 Taiwanese tractor. Near Taitung, 1965. Girl of sixteen ploughing a hemp field with a simple wooden plough and a water buffalo. In the tropics there are no seasons in the Western sense; thus there are ripe crops next door to freshly tilled fields.

54 Eels and octopus. Pusan, Korea, 1953. Next to agriculture, fishing is the most important industry of Korea, involving one million people and furnishing one-sixth of the national product.

55 Fishmonger in Pusan, Korea, 1953. The scarcity of arable land makes Korea a country practically without large domestic animals. The diet contains hardly any meat; eighty-five per cent of all animal protein is provided by fish.

56 Korean dancer and musician. Seoul, 1953. Dancers are equally skilled in playing the thousand-year-old kayakum, a large zither, similar to the Japanese koto.

57 It's all clean again. Seoul, Korea, 1965. Laundry is done in the river, winter and summer. The heavy wet garments have to be carried back, often more than half a mile, one of the heavy chores of the housewife.

58 Suwon, a fifteenth-century capital of Korea nineteen miles south of Seoul. 1953. A pleasure pavilion of the period overlooks the city outskirts, with vegetable gardens on the slopes and rice fields in the plain.

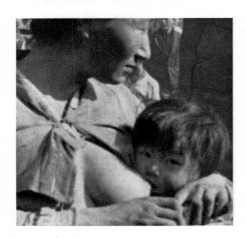

59 After the fire. Pusan, the only big Korean city which was spared from bombing and street fighting in two years of war, was ravaged by fire one Saturday in November, 1953. Half the city was destroyed in one night. This picture was taken the following day. While the ashes were still hot all the people started rebuilding their homes.

60 Harvest in the Naktong valley, South Korea, 1952. Korea is a predominantly agricultural country. Four out of five people are members of farm families. Half the farms are under two and a half acres, a third are less than one acre. The main crops are rice and barley. Rice is the staple diet; barley, ripening three months earlier, carries the family over until the new harvest.

39

61 Only turnips to sell in winter. Farmer's family at the market. Pusan, Korea, winter, 1952.

62 Bringing in the potato crop, Han river valley, 1964. In Korea it is rare to find such large areas planted with potatoes.

63 Han river valley, Korea, 1964. Farmhouses are surrounded by a wall or a stout fence, creating a farmyard around the porch where threshing and winnowing are done at harvest time and where, near the house in giant earthenware jars, the pickles (kim-chi) are stored; these form an essential part of the Korean diet.

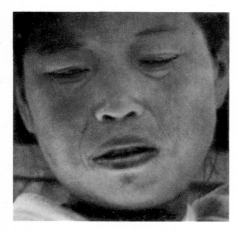

64 Market in Pusan, Korea, 1953. Korean mothers carrying their babies wear this practical loose blouse ('Tshagori'), which allows them to switch the baby round from the back to feed it without loss of time during work.

65 Rice harvest near Pusan, Korea, autumn 1953. Women don't wear jewellery in Korea, nor embroidered or fancy dresses. Skirts of heavy home-made silk in beautiful muted but vivid colours are worn for work just as on Sunday.

66 A time for meditation. Pusan, Korea, 1953. Service in a Confucian temple. Upper left, the Korean flag which features the old Chinese symbol of life. Confucianism, more a philosophy than a religion, manifests the greatest simplicity in architecture and decoration.

67 Midwifery training course. Seoul, Korea, 1956. Practising midwives, all married and with children of their own, in a government-sponsored refresher course to acquaint them with new methods. They often have to travel many miles on bicycle to perform a delivery.

68 Goodbye, Mother! Pusan, Korea, 1953. Funeral. The woman supporting herself on two sticks, wailing loudly, is following the coffin of her mother. It was taken from the house and carried in procession with banners and chants up into the hills for burial—a distance of several miles. Male members of the family and friends follow immediately behind the coffin, the women further back. Like everyone else, the daughter is dressed in hemp ('straw cloth'), and around head and waist she wears a straw rope braided counter-clockwise. The ceremony lasts hours, so the baby is brought along.

41

69 Old dances in new Korea. Kyongbok Palace, Seoul, 1965. Dance is an important part of Korean cultural heritage. It goes back more than a thousand years. It is reported that in A.D. 1400 eight hundred dancers and musicians were part of the Emperor's retinue. In 1494 all details of costumes, music, instruments, etc., were recorded in the *Akhak Kwaebun*. Young ladies revive the old tradition in kaesang costumes, accompanied by the big hourglass-shaped drum and the kayakum (Korean koto).

70 Asleep in the nest. Pusan, Korea, 1952. Korean mothers carry their babies for two years comfortably tied to their backs with a blanket, sometimes longer if no sibling has arrived. I have often thought that the striking self-assurance of the Koreans in a world of worries and material problems stems from these first years in complete security.

71 Biscuits for sale, baby has eaten. Pusan, Korea, 1952. In Korea hardly any cows' milk is available, thus babies are often breast fed until the age of four.

72 How to dig a well. Asakusa, Tokyo, 1954. Five women in their blue-printed cotton kimonos, their heads covered with towels, draw the ropes in rhythmic movements to the chants, hand-clapping and stamping of a female 'foreman'.

73 Young Japanese ground stewardess.
Tokyo Airport, 1964.

74 Toshogu shrine in Nikko, Japan, 1956. Young
girls of about fourteen to sixteen years of age enter
Shinto temples for a few years, then go back into
normal life. Some return to the temple decades later
to finish their days. They are called Miko. Their duty
covers any kind of practical work, like helping in the
temple, sweeping the floor or, as here, selling prayers
and Buddha prints as souvenirs.

75 Tokyo nightclub, 1966. Half-Asian actress (either
Eurasian or, more likely, Afro-Asian) in a revue at
the Nichigeki Theatre. Japanese of mixed blood are
often of unusual beauty. In spite of this, they are
outcasts in Japan just as race mixtures are in the
southern United States.

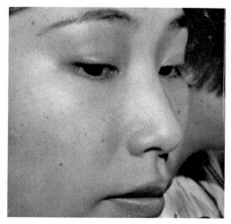

76 Switchboard operator. Japan, 1958. Telephone
office in Fuji City at the foot of Fujiyama.

43

77 Resting pilgrim. Shikoku, Japan, 1964. Woman pilgrim resting on a street corner, wearing appropriate garb; leg bindings, leather shoes with separated big toe to allow the strapping on of wooden clogs, Cellophane-covered straw hat. Men and women make long, strenuous journeys, often for a whole year, braving the hardships of winter and summer, sleeping in temples. The ultimate goal is the total grasp of reality, manifest in the landscape and its seasonal changes.

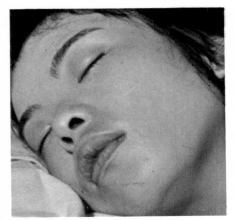

78 Sleeping Japanese girl.

79 At the Fifth Station of Fujiyama, 1960. Innkeeper at Gogome. Every summer one hundred thousand people climb the beautiful sacred mountain of Japan for pleasure and as a pilgrimage. Eight stations on the way to the top allow rest and simple meals. This station, the fifth, is nearly seven thousand feet up at 'the borderline between Earth and Heaven', where vegetation stops.

80 Shiratsuka, Japan, 1956. Along the coast between Tokyo and Shizuoka meagre pines line the shore, exactly as Hiroshige painted it in his famous woodcut series of the Tokaido Highway in 1834. A farm woman in a blue cotton dress is weeding a field of sweet potatoes.

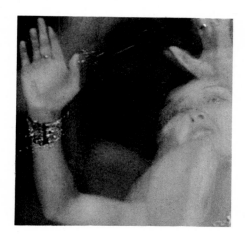

81 Nightclub performer on the tight-rope. Nichigeki Theatre, Tokyo, 1953.

82 and 83 The threshing is done. Odawara, Japan, 1966. Farmer's wife on her way home from the fields. Straw mat and rope are implements for winnowing.

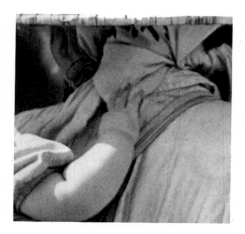

84 Watching the world from a train window. Japan, 1965.

45

The Photographs

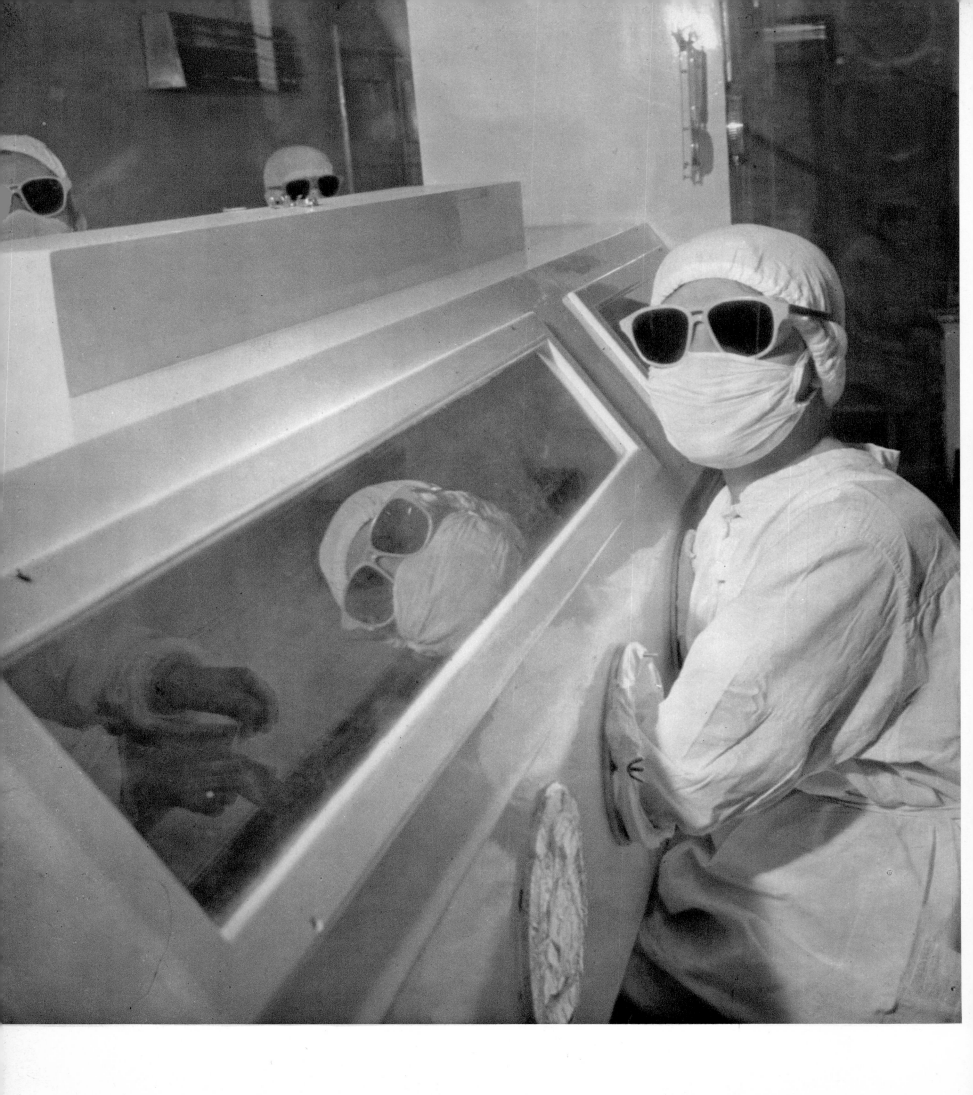

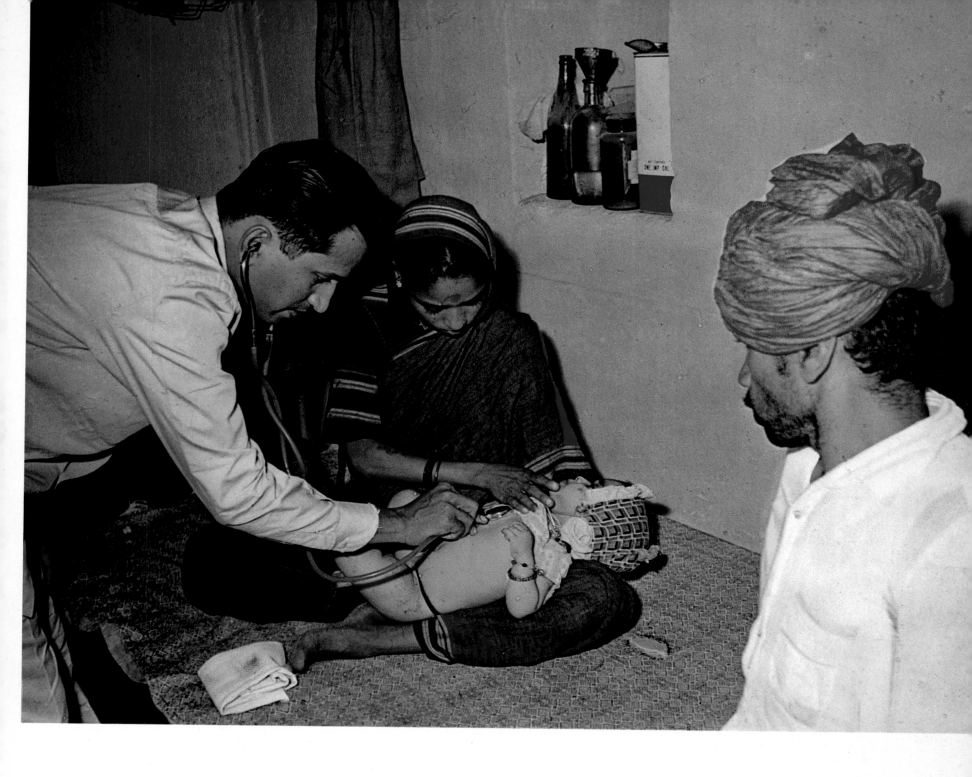

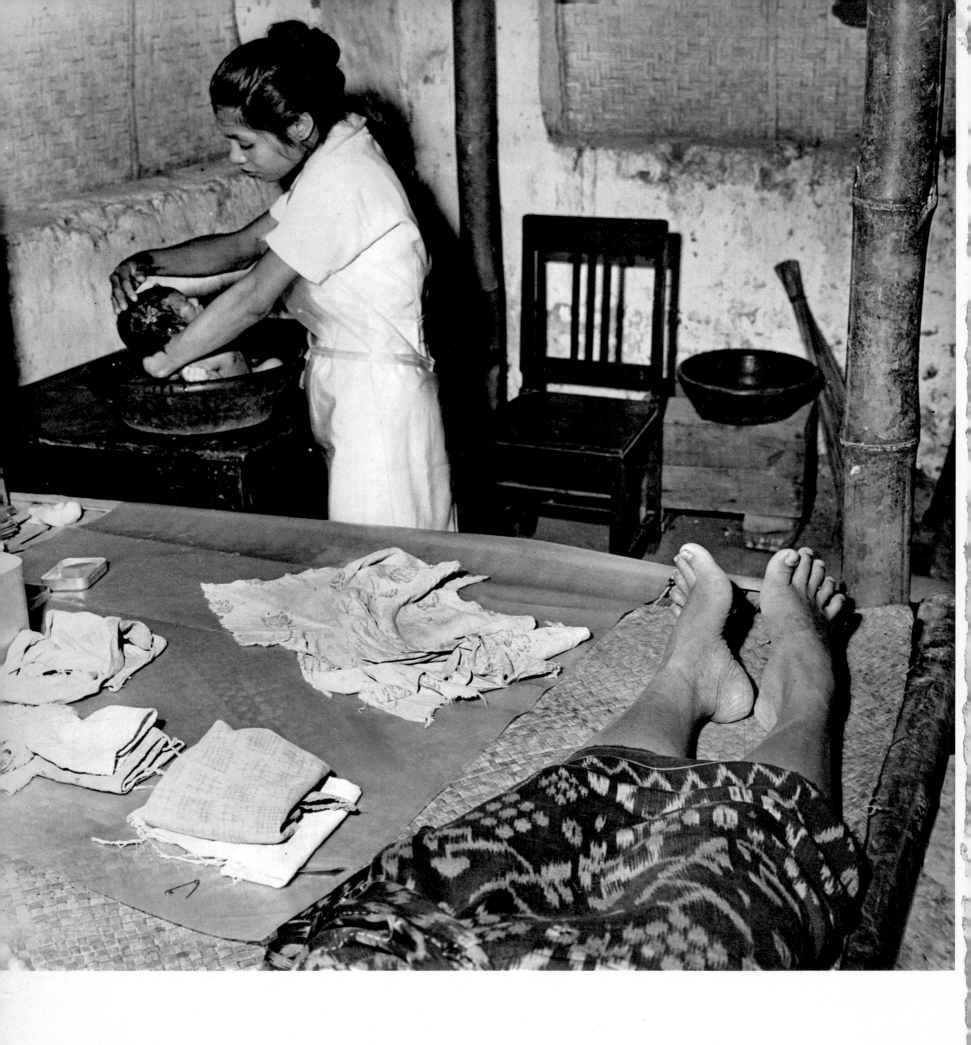

29

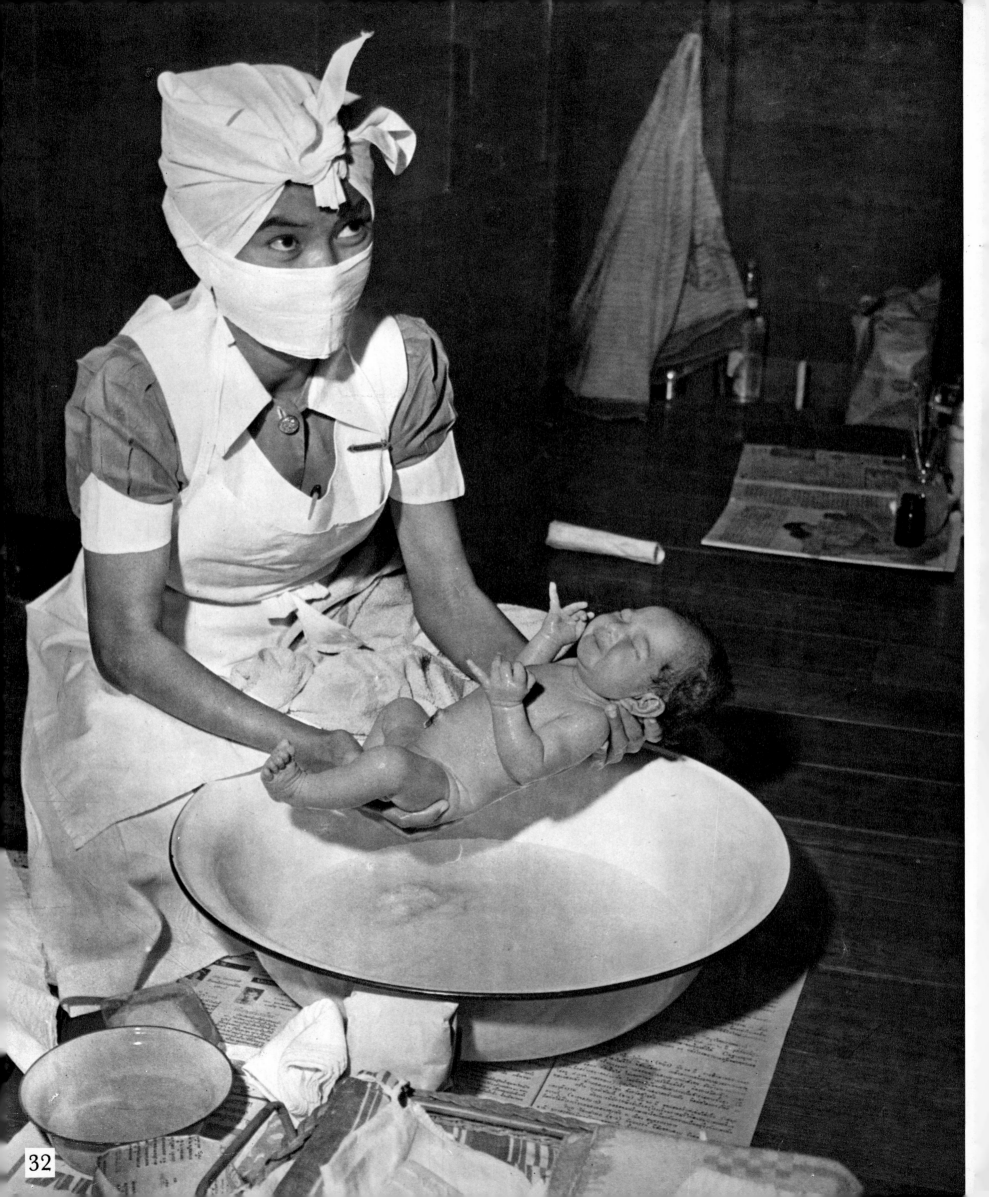

33

37

43

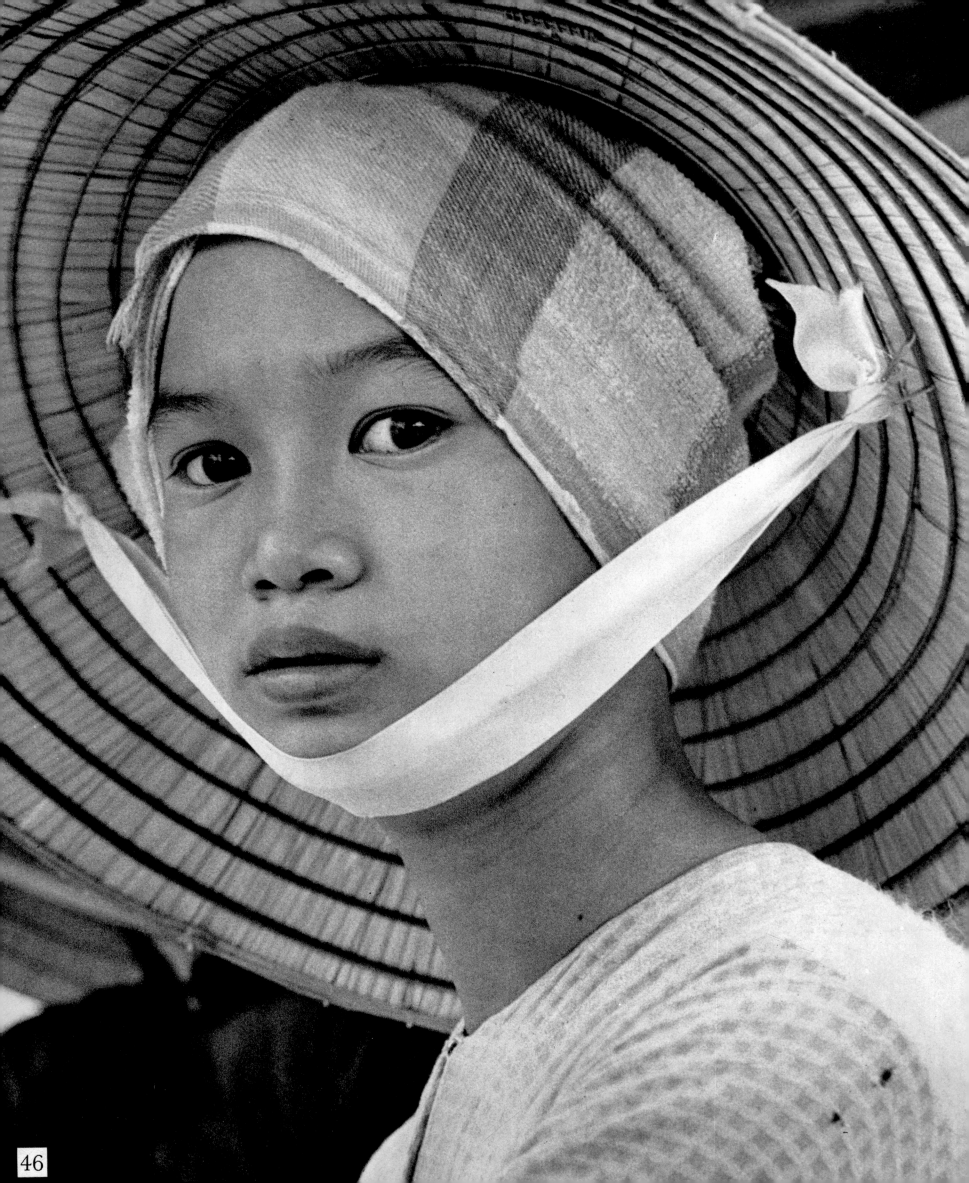